POWER CHORDS

To access audio visit:
www.halleonard.com/mylibrary

Enter Code
5978-1395-8577-2432

ISBN 978-0-634-05789-8

HAL•LEONARD®
7777 W. BLUEMOUND RD. P.O. BOX 13819 MILWAUKEE, WI 53213

CONTENTS

CHAPTER FOUR

CHAPTER FIVE

CHAPTER SIX

APPENDIX

INTRODUCTION

The power chord is the signature sound of rock 'n' roll guitar. Almost all the great rock 'n' roll songs, past and present, are built on that wide-open, no-nonsense sonic foundation. Not only are power chords mighty and rebellious, they're also incredibly convenient. With just a few simple fingerings, you can access thousands of songs.

In this book, we'll examine how various power chords are constructed, and how they've been used in context—from early rock 'n' roll standards, to 1960s British Invasion songs, to '70s punk, to '80s "hair metal," to '90s grunge, and beyond. Popular songs from all these eras, as well as new examples "in the style of," are included. When you've finished this book, you should be able to play these songs and understand the concepts behind them, and you'll also know how to invent your own power-chord moves; in short, you'll be ready to rock.

A Note to Beginners

This book is geared toward guitarists with some experience on the instrument, but it can also serve as a great introduction to rock guitar for the absolute beginner. Just listen closely to the audio as you learn the examples, and make good use of the appendix—it contains fretboard diagrams, a guitar notation manual, tips on reading chord diagrams and tablature, and more.

Take it slowly. If any of the examples are too fast, learn them at a slower pace with a metronome (some are played as slow demos on the track). Once you have a tune down in a slow and steady groove, it will take no time to get up to speed.

The first track contains the guitar's notes in standard tuning:

TRACK 1 TUNING NOTES: E–A–D–G–B–E

CHAPTER 1

What Is a Power Chord?

Even if you're not an experienced musician, you can probably hear the difference between major and minor chords. You might sense that one sounds "light" and another sounds "dark." When you hear these chords, you're usually hearing a combination of three different notes—the *root*, *3rd*, and *5th* (the first, third, and fifth notes of a scale). What makes a chord major or minor is where you put the *3rd*; throw it out, and you've got a **power chord**.

A power chord, also known as a "five" chord, has just two essential notes—the *root* and *fifth* notes of a scale. In most scales, these notes are three and a half steps apart, or the equivalent of eight frets on the guitar. Here is a C major scale, with the pitches numbered:

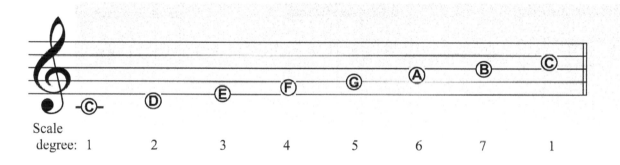

Take the root (C) and fifth (G) notes of the C major scale, and you have the most basic version of a "C5" power chord.

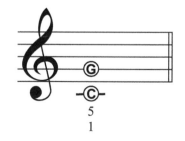

Wherever there's a power chord in a piece of music, you'll see the letter name of the chord's root and the suffix "5"—e.g., C5. Don't worry about playing this yet—just understand what it looks like and how it relates to the scale.

Open Power Chords

Open power chords are played in open position—that is, at the bottom of the guitar neck, using open strings. As shown below, many two-note, open-position power chords—E5, A5, and D5—have the same fingering shape, using only one left-hand finger. The root note is played as an open string, and each 5th is fretted by the index finger on the 2nd fret of the higher string.

Play the E5, A5, and D5 frames, and make sure you strum only the two strings of the chord. Notice the different sounds of these chords; even though music is an aural language, guitarists can be guilty of relying more on their eyes and fingers than their ears!

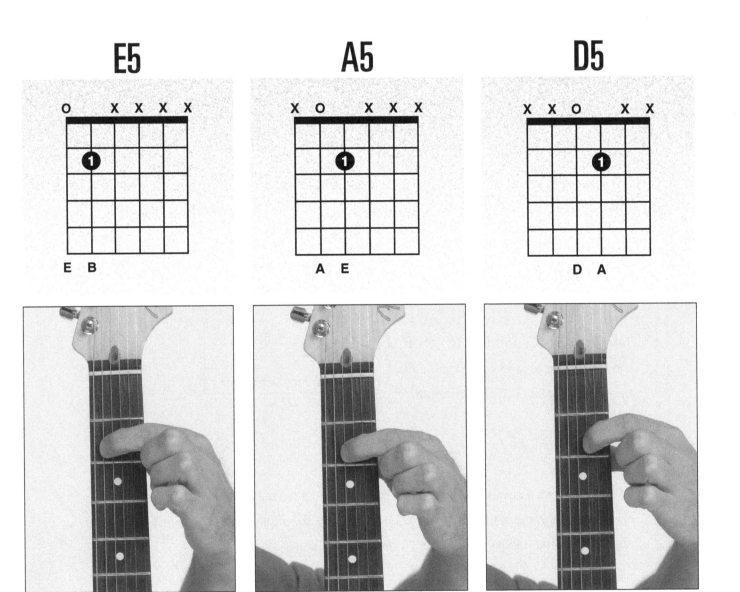

E5   A5   D5

O X X X X X   X O X X X   X X O X X

E B   A E   D A

Once you're acquainted with these three power chords, let's check them out in context. Here's a simple hard rock progression, similar to one you might hear from AC/DC.

Play this example—and all others—along with the audio to get the proper rhythm. The *repeat signs* (‖: :‖) call for all the music to be played again—play up to the end, then go back to the first repeat sign and play again from there.

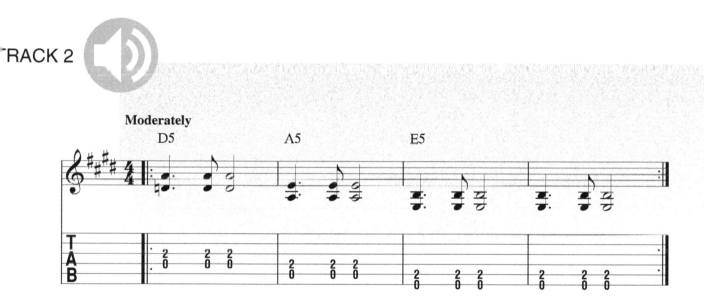

When you move your fret-hand index finger for each chord, try not to brush against unwanted strings. With your pick hand, strike each pair of strings with just enough force to let the chords ring clearly, and try not to hit the strings too hard. That works in some situations, but too much force on these low chords will make them sound out of tune. It can also break your strings!

Three-Note Voicings

The power chords we've seen so far can be expanded into *three-note voicings*. In these, each root note is reinforced with the same note one octave (12 half steps) higher, for a fuller sound.

The E5 and A5 chords can be played with a variation of the same fingering you've been using: keep your index finger on the 5th as before, and straighten it out to *bar* (simultaneously fret) the octave at the second fret:

E5

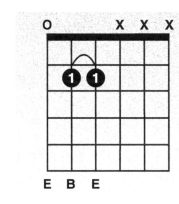

A5

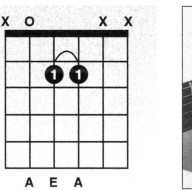

For the D5 chord, put your index finger on the third string, second fret A (as before), and the ring finger on the second string, third fret D:

D5

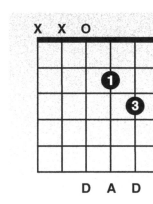

Here's an alternate fingering for the E5 chord:

Fret with the middle and ring fingers on the fifth (B) and octave (E), respectively.

Use whichever fingering is more comfortable for you on the next example.

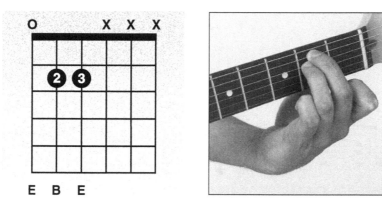

While fretting all these new shapes, play the notes individually, and make sure that each one rings out clearly. Compare the sounds of these three-note chords to the two-note versions. Then try this version of the hard rock progression with three-note voicings. Notice how much fuller they sound?

TRACK 3

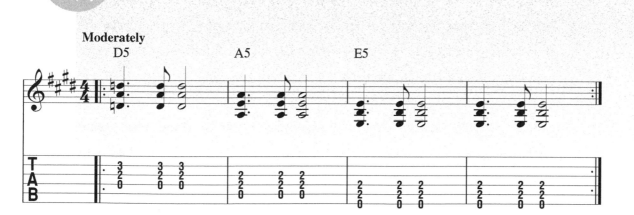

Single-Note Lines

Guitarists often spice up power-chord progressions with single-note lines. Here's a version of the same hard rock progression with added single notes in a groovy rhythm. A slow demo follows.

TRACK 4

To play the example, fret the D5 shape and strike it once. Keep holding the chord, and pick the open fourth string again, then play the same string on the fourth fret with your pinky finger. (If your pinky is disagreeable, you can fret the D5 chord with your index and middle fingers on the third and second strings, then use your ring finger for the fourth-fret F♯.)

As you hit the open fifth string on beat 4, fret the open A5 shape (always think ahead), and in the next measure, use your ring finger to fret the fourth-fret C♯. Use the same one-finger shape for the E5 chord; that way, you can leave the chord fretted while you play the third-fret G♮ and the fourth-fret G♯ with your middle and ring fingers, respectively.

Notice the soulful quality added by these single-note lines? The G♮ played after the E5 chord is a *flatted third*, also known as a "blue note"—an essential element in blues and rock.

Arpeggios

Power chords—and any other chords—can also be played as *arpeggios*, that is, one note at a time. Here's our familiar progression played in arpeggios.

TRACK 5

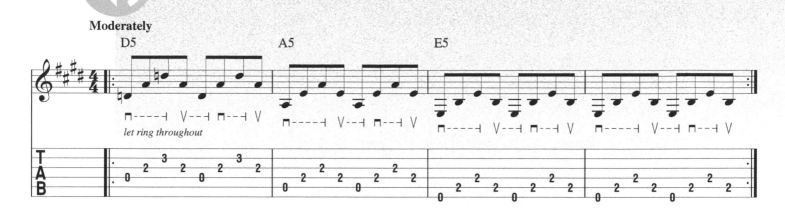

Pick the notes as shown in the picking pattern below the staff; the staple-looking symbol represents a *downstroke* (toward the floor), and the "V" symbolizes an *upstroke* (toward the ceiling). Keep your fret-hand fingers held down on each chord shape for as long as possible, and let all the notes ring out.

Now let's check out a couple well-known songs with open-position power chords and single-note lines. "Ramrod," first recorded by Duane Eddy in 1958, is based on open A5 and D5 chords. Those single-note bass lines in between the chords include the ♭3 blue note (on fret 3) and the lower fifth (the open string). Hold down each chord for as long as possible while fretting each third-fret note with your middle finger, then lift your finger for the open-string note.

TRACK 6

Ramrod

Fast Rock ♩ = 165   Words and Music by Al Casey

In Van Halen's version of "You Really Got Me," Eddie Van Halen alternates between a G note and an A5 chord, adding special techniques, detailed below, that are rock guitar staples. You'll see some major differences between this version and the Kinks' original later.

You Really Got Me

TRACK 7

Words and Music by Ray Davies

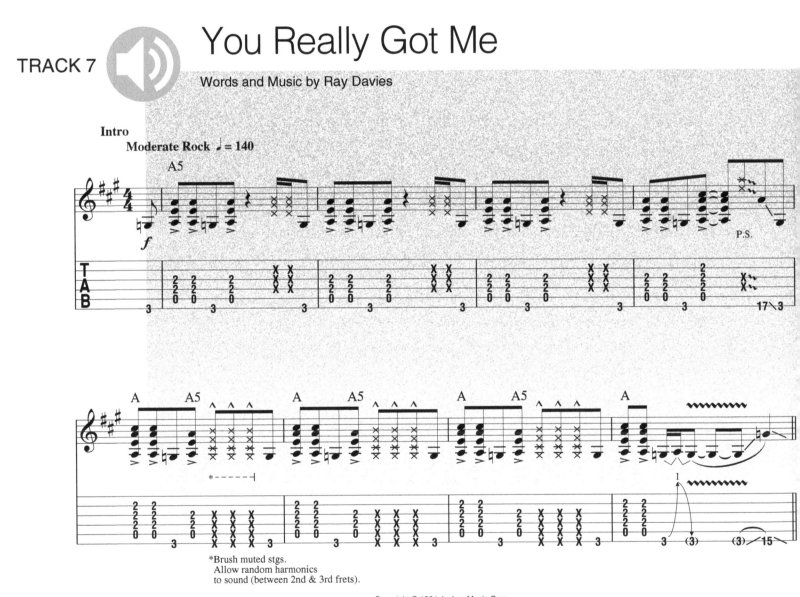

*Brush muted stgs.
Allow random harmonics
to sound (between 2nd & 3rd frets).

The X's in notation and tablature show *fret-hand muting*—a percussive technique that's common in funk and rock. To produce this muffled sound, just release fret-hand pressure, but keep your hand laid over the strings so they don't ring out. Give the muted strings a quick back-and-forth swipe with the pick, then return to the G–A5 pattern.

The A5 turns into an A major chord in measure 4, when the pick-hand barre is extended to cover the B string on the second fret. Then comes a *pick scrape* (P.S.)—run the edge of the pick down the strings with your right hand—followed by a left-hand slide. The pattern continues with alternating A major and A5 chords, but the mutes become eighth-note punches with *random harmonics*—the high overtones you'll hear when your muting hand sits lightly between the second and third frets.

A one-step *bend and release* falls on beat 2 of the last measure. Play the G note with your middle finger and pull it down (toward the floor) until it sounds a whole step higher, the equivalent of an open A note. Then release it back to G and add some vibrato (pivot your wrist quickly to make the string "warble"). Next comes another flashy slide: just keep your finger pressed down while you run it up and down the sixth string.

How about some more open power chords? Here's a conventional G5 fingering.

Notice that the index finger (or the side of the middle finger) mutes the fifth string—just lay it on the string; don't push down.

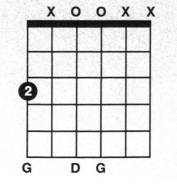

Here are two fingerings for an open-position C5 chord. The first is a two-note voicing: The middle finger frets the chord's root, and the fourth string is muted with the first finger (shown), ring finger, or the side of the middle finger.

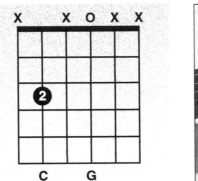

Here's the three-note C5 voicing. It adds an octave on the second string to reinforce the root. Mute the fourth string with the side of your ring finger while it frets the root note.

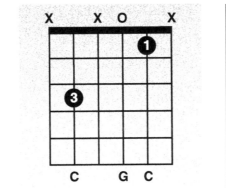

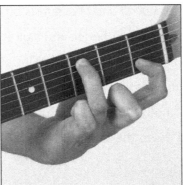

Now try a progression that includes open C5, D5, and G5 chords. The G5 in this example includes another fifth added on the second string. Fret this note with your ring finger.

TRACK 8

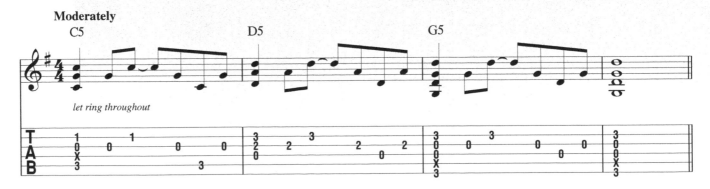

Here's an example that uses all the open power chords you've learned so far—A5, C5, D5, E5, and G5—and some special techniques: palm muting, arpeggios, and bends. A slow version follows on the track.

TRACK 9

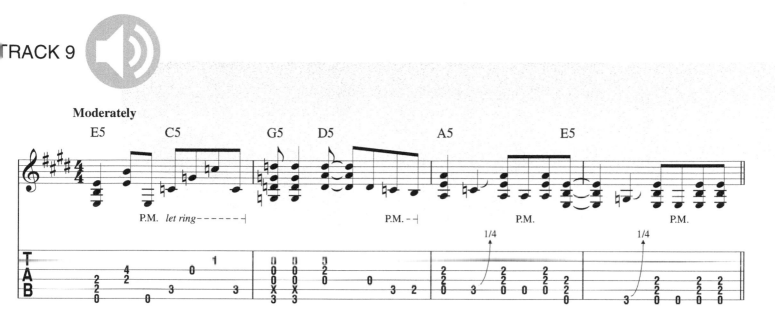

Use the one-finger E5 chord shape on this one. Note that the G5 and D5 chords share the same D note on string 2, fret 3. In the interest of efficiency, keep your ring finger on that note as you switch between chords.

Notice the *palm mutes* (marked "P.M.") in this pattern. While you pick, just rest the back of your pick-hand palm on the strings where they meet the bridge. So the notes sound in tune, don't push down too hard—just enough to get that "chunk" sound.

On the beat 2 of measures 3 and 4, the arrow and the label "1/4" calls for a slight bend, less than a half step. Pull the string downward *slightly* with your middle finger.

Now, with your newfound power-chord knowledge, try creating some of your own riffs. Experiment with the techniques we've covered: fret-hand and palm muting, single-note slurs, and bends. Strive for creativity, and document your riffs by writing them out on manuscript paper or recording them.

CHAPTER 2
Moveable Power Chords (Strings 6–5)

Because of the parallel layout of the guitar's strings, you can use one fingering to play many *moveable* (or *closed position*) power chords all over the fretboard. Start with this shape: fret any sixth-string note with your index finger, and with your ring finger, fret the fifth-string note that is two frets higher. You can use your pinky finger on the fifth string too, but using the ring finger will give you more flexibility when special techniques come into play.

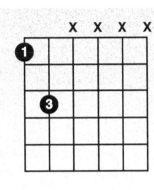

Now let's start with an open, two-note E5 chord, then climb chromatically (via half steps) to a twelfth-fret E5 chord. Fret the first E5 chord normally, then use the fingering above for the remaining chords. As you play each chord, say its name.

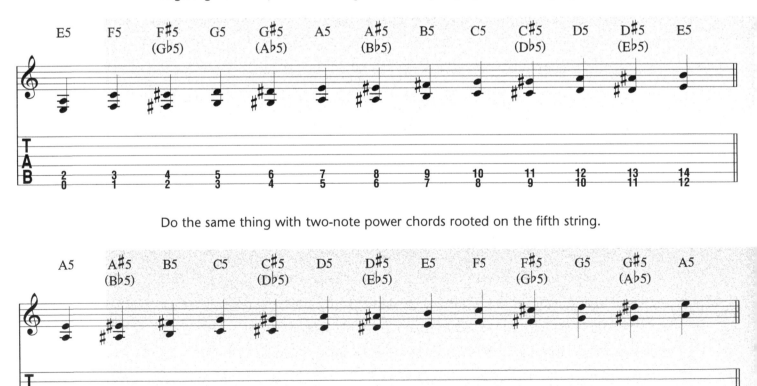

Do the same thing with two-note power chords rooted on the fifth string.

No book on power chords would be complete without the ominous "Iron Man" riff. Black Sabbath guitarist Tony Iommi played it exclusively with two-note, sixth-string-root power chords.

Iron Man

Words and Music by Frank Iommi, John Osbourne, William Ward and Terence Butler

When slides (the diagonal lines on the staff) are shown by themselves, they represent a *position shift*. After you strike the first B5 chord, slide up to the next chord without lifting your fret-hand fingers. The next set of slides—between the D5 and E5 chords, and surrounded by arches—are *legato slides*. After you strike the D5, slide up to the E5 without picking. Measure 2 has the opposite move: a *downward* legato slide between the G5 and F#5 chords. Listen to the track for the desired result.

You can also play the "Iron Man" riff with a combination of fifth- and sixth-string-root power chords:

Eric Clapton's "Layla" riff features fifth-string-root power chords, flanked by single-note lines from the D natural minor scale (D–E–F–G–A–B♭–C). A slow demo follows on the track.

TRACK 11

Layla

Words and Music by Eric Clapton and Jim Gordon

The opening single-note lick revolves around *hammer-ons* and *pull-offs*. Pick the first open A, then *hammer on* the next C note (fret it without picking). Pick the next open D and quickly hammer on the F note at the third fret, then *pull* your finger *off* the string without picking. Note the legato slide from D5 to C5, and the position-shift slide from the last D5 back to the lick.

Three-Note Moveable Power Chords

Like open power chords, moveable power chords are often played as three-note voicings. These common fingerings can be used for both fifth- and sixth-string-root power chords.

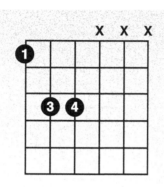

The second shape includes a ring-finger barre; make sure that the top two notes ring out clearly.

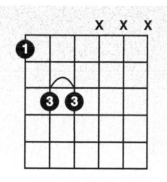
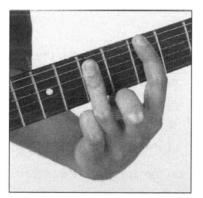

In a less common fingering, the pinky finger bars the highest notes.

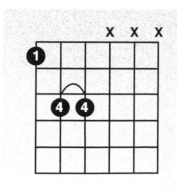

Now let's check out some three-note moveable power chords in context. From the British Invasion era, The Kinks' original "You Really Got Me" features sixth-string-root F5 and G5 chords. (Compare this to the Van Halen version you learned earlier, which uses open-position power chords in the key of A.)

TRACK 12

You Really Got Me

Words and Music by Ray Davies

Recorded two decades later, the Scorpions' "Rock You Like a Hurricane" includes three-note power chords rooted on both the 5th and 6th strings.

This riff is full of *syncopation*: certain chords are accented on the *upbeats* (or the "ands" of the beats). Be sure to play the first G5 and D5 chords, and the C5 chord, on the appropriate upbeats.

TRACK 13

Rock You Like a Hurricane

Words and Music by Herman Rarebell, Klaus Meine and Rudolf Schenker

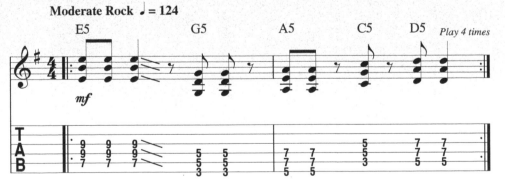

Try this power pop-inspired progression with chords rooted on the fifth and sixth strings. Play it all in downstrokes. Note the cool syncopation formed by alternating full chord stabs and palm-muted roots.

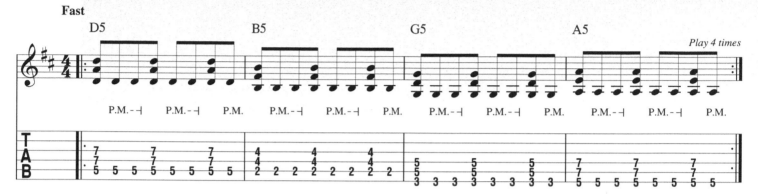

You can also try playing the figure with roots all along the sixth string; the D5 and B5 chords will be played with your index finger on the root at frets 10 and 7, respectively.

The must-know grunge riff for "Smells Like Teen Spirit" strays outside the realm of the 5 chord. Nirvana's Kurt Cobain bars the chords' higher notes with his ring finger, and "accidentally" strikes a note above each power chord, resulting in sus4 and major chords. To get the muted scratches (X's) between chords, lift your fret-hand fingers off the frets, but keep them laid over the strings.

There's a neat chord-switching trick on the "and" of each beat 4: Cobain strums open strings as he shifts chord shapes, maintaining momentum and adding extra "grunge."

Smells Like Teen Spirit

Words and Music by Kurt Cobain, Chris Novoselic and David Grohl

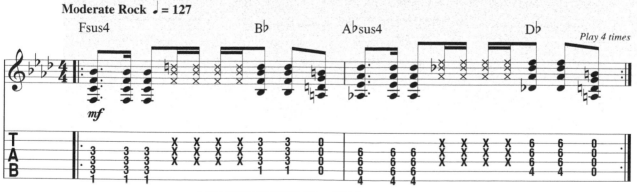

Chromaticism

The chord progressions we've played so far have been mostly *diatonic*, that is, occurring within the song's key. Now let's check out some *chromatic* applications of power chords, commonly seen in metal progressions like this one:

TRACK 16

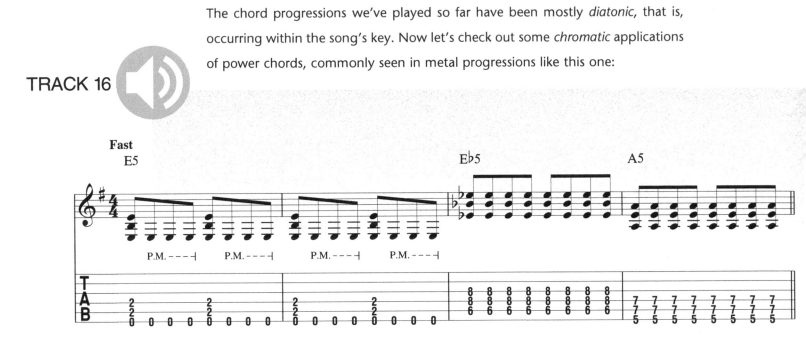

The third measure features an E♭5 chord, in which all the pitches are foreign to the key of E minor. The E♭5 moves to an A5 in the next measure. The roots of these two chords are a *tritone* (♯4 or ♭5) apart. That interval—known in olden days as the "devil in music"—produces an ominous heavy-metal sound. In a dark room, play the E♭5–A5 sequence over and over. Scared?

Here is another progression that features an "outside" chord; the B♭5 is a tritone away from the tonic, E. The riff's sinister quality is compounded by palm mutes on the open 6th string.

TRACK 17

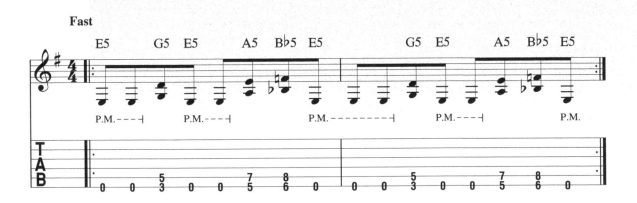

Now try playing some other tritone progressions: C5–G♭5, G5–D♭5, etc.

Chromatic applications of power chords are not limited to metal; below is a country-rock example in the key of G major. Try it with slight distortion.

TRACK 18

In the first measure, the diatonic C5 and D5 chords are connected by a chromatic C#5 chord. The C#5 chord also slides into the D5 chord on beat 4, as shown by *grace notes* and played quickly before the beat (an embellishment often used in country). In the third measure, an F#5 chord similarly connects F5 and G5 chords. For the fingerings of the single-note fills, refer to the numbers beneath the tab staves. ("3" = ring finger; "1" = index finger.)

Before you move on to the next chapter, make sure you're comfortable playing power chords rooted on the fifth and sixth strings. Can you instantly finger any given power chord? Try shifting the fingerings of this chapter's riffs; for example, if a figure has both fifth- and sixth-string root chords, try playing them all on the sixth string. Then invent a few new power-chord figures of your own.

CHAPTER 3
More Moveable Power Chords (Strings 4–3)

Two-note chords rooted on the fourth string have the same fingering as those rooted on the fifth and sixth strings: the index finger frets the root, while the ring finger frets the 5th. Three-note chords with a fourth-string root require a new fingering: the pinky frets the reinforced root a fret higher than before.

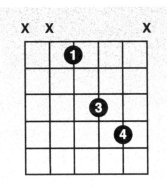

Now play all the fourth-string-root power chords up to the twelfth fret. Say the names of the chords as you ascend the fretboard; for good measure, descend, too.

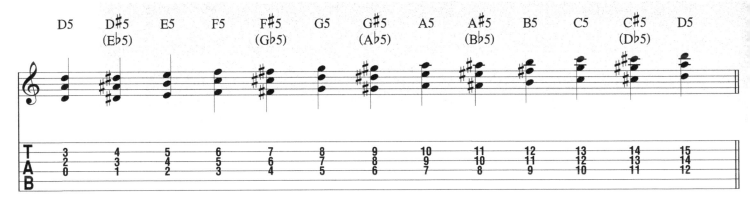

TRACK 19

Now try this simple A5–F5–G5 progression using the same chord shape:

Moderately fast

Ozzy's Osbourne's killer "Bark at the Moon" riff, created by guitarist Jake E. Lee, includes several fourth-string-root chords, alternated with the palm-muted open fifth string. In the first full measure, an A5 chord appears every 1½ beats. This creates a *hemiola* effect, or a feeling of three beats against four.

TRACK 20

Bark at the Moon

Words and Music by Ozzy Osbourne

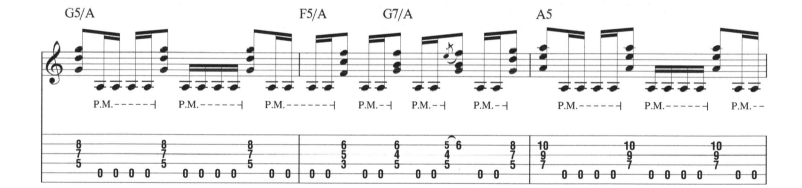

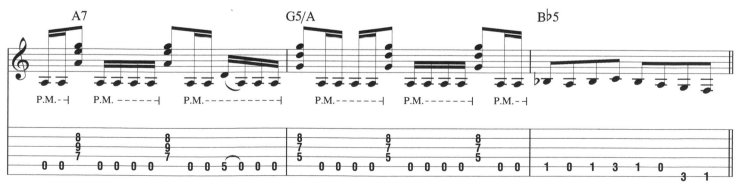

To learn the riff, let's isolate one chord and concentrate on the picking pattern. Use alternate picking on the palm-muted pitches, as shown below. Pick from your wrist (as opposed to your fingers), and gradually work your way up to the brisk tempo of 148 bpm.

TRACK 21

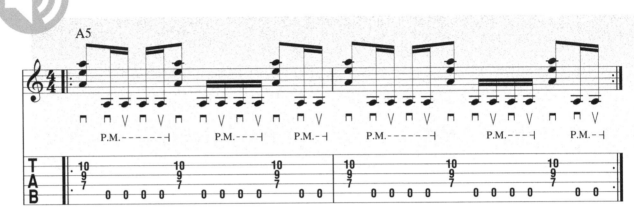

Once you have this basic picking pattern down, try playing the entire riff. Again, slowly work up to the song's fast tempo.

For two-note chords with a third-string root, there's another new fingering: the index finger frets the root, while the pinky finger frets the 5th, located three frets higher on the second string.

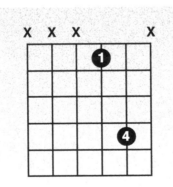
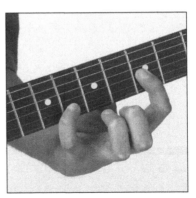

For three-note power chords with third-string roots, you need to bar the higher notes with the pinky finger. This fingering might seem awkward, but conditioning the pinky finger will help strengthen your lead work.

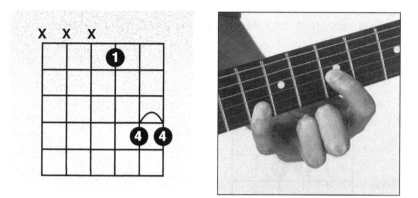

Here's a pop pattern built on a series of third-string-root power chord arpeggios. Make sure that all notes ring for as long as possible—you only need to switch positions on each first, third, and fourth beat. Strive for smooth transitions from chord to chord.

RACK 22

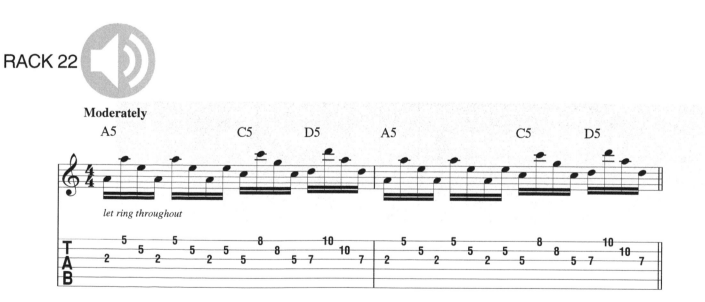

Expanded Open Power Chords

Now that your pinky's in action, let's look at open power chords again. Take the new fingering you just learned and move it to the second fret. Shift your index finger to the fourth string, and straighten it out to bar the fourth and third strings on fret 2. Keep your pinky on fret 5, strings 1 and 2, add the open 5th string, and you have a thick, five-note A5 chord, spelled A–E–A–E–A. You can look at this as an expanded version of the first A5 shape you learned in Chapter 1.

A5

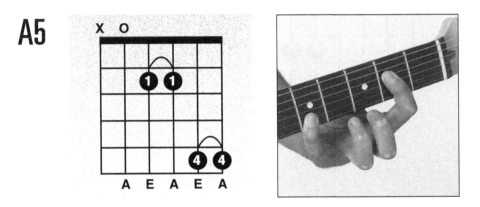

You can also expand an open D5 power chord with the pinky finger on the first string, fifth fret A:

D5

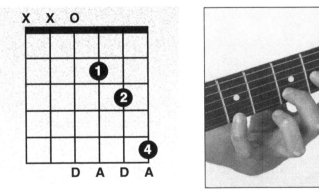

Now try expanding an open E5 chord with the open first and second strings. Start with a conventional open E major chord, as shown. Release pressure on your index finger, so that the third string is muted, and strum all the strings.

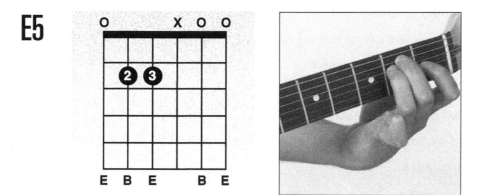

E5

E B E B E

Here's an "arena rock" progression that uses our new chords. Take this one slowly, so you can switch evenly between the new voicings. Also, use your pinky finger to fret the quarter-step bends; that way, you can keep the E5 chord down.

RACK 23

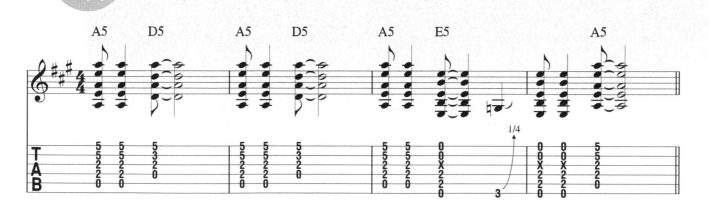

Even More Moveable Power Chords (Strings 2–1)

Two-note power chords rooted on the second string have the same fingering as those rooted on strings 4–6: the index finger frets the root; the ring finger frets the 5th. Because these chords are in the guitar's higher range, they're better for lead work than accompaniment.

This next passage uses second-string-root power chords in a sliding E minor riff inspired by Jimi Hendrix. Try it with a clean tone, and let the open sixth string ring throughout.

TRACK 24

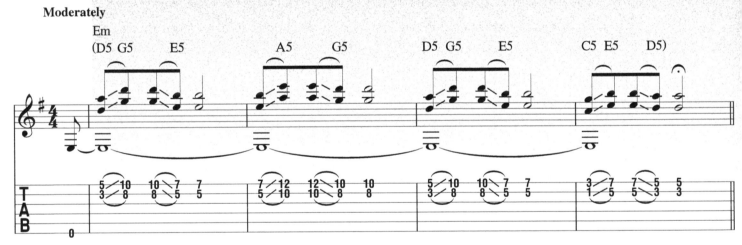

That bellybutton-looking symbol above the last chord is a *fermata*; this tells you to hold the chord for longer than its given value (in this case, a half note). You'll see this wherever chords are meant to ring out on song endings.

Now, with power chords rooted on the fourth, third, and second strings, experiment with some of your own riffs. Also, tinker with the fattened open power chords we've covered.

CHAPTER 4
Power Chords in Inversion

Any power chord can be played in *inversion*, that is, with a note other than the root (for our purposes, the 5th) as its lowest note. This can add a thicker, darker sound to your power chord voicings.

Let's start with a three-note open D5 chord:

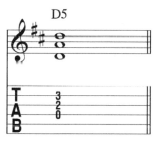

To add its lower 5th (A), simply include the open fifth string. What results is called a D5/A. This is known as a *slash chord*; the symbol to the left is the main chord, and the letter to the right is the bass note.

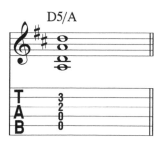

Randy Rhoads' riffing in Ozzy's "Flying High Again" features this new chord, and also a G5/A chord—a G5 played above an open fifth string A.

Flying High Again

TRACK 24

Words and Music by Ozzy Osbourne, Randy Rhoads, Bob Daisley and Lee Kerslake

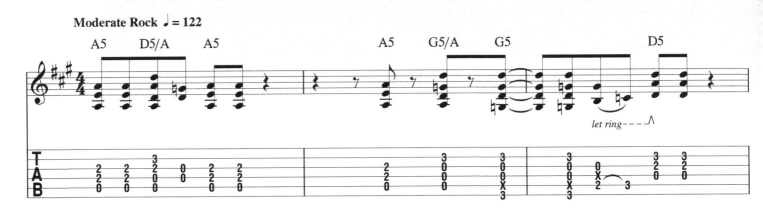

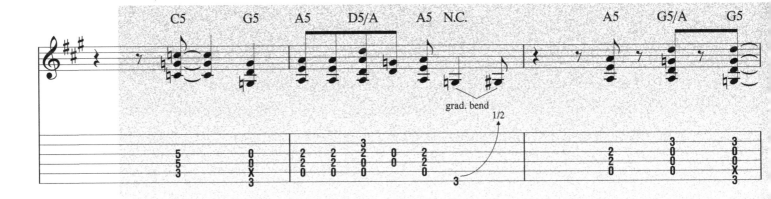

Now let's try a moveable power chord inversion. Fret a three-note C5 chord, and bar the fifth and sixth strings at the third fret to add a low G. Here are two fingerings for this chord:

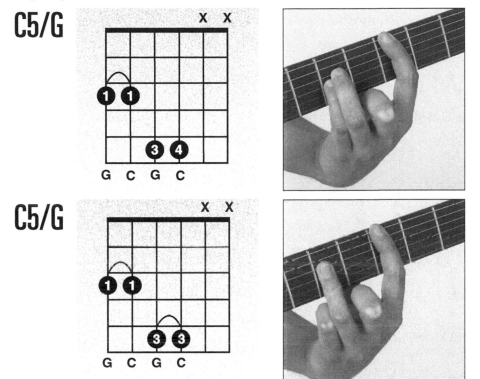

As you did with earlier chords, try moving the fingering chromatically up to the twelfth fret—start with the first-fret B♭5/F, move to the second-fret B5/F♯, and so on. Name each chord along the way.

Weezer's "Hash Pipe" also uses this inversion. The first two measures involve D5/A and E5/B chords. Measures 3–4 introduce a "spy theme" with regular B5 and C5 chords pitted against an open A string.

TRACK 26 ## Hash Pipe

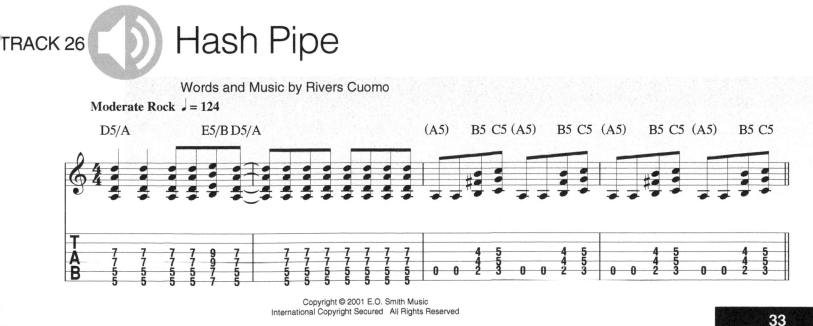

Trevor Rabin of Yes plays the "Owner of a Lonely Heart" progression with an open A5 chord and various moveable power chords. The B5/F and C5/G inversions in measures 1 and 2 create a thickening effect for the opening, then it settles into straight three-note moveable power chords for the rest of the intro. Watch for the palm mutes on the G5 chords.

Owner of a Lonely Heart

Intro
Moderately ♩ = 125

Words and Music by Trevor Horn, Jon Anderson, Trevor Rabin and Chris Squire

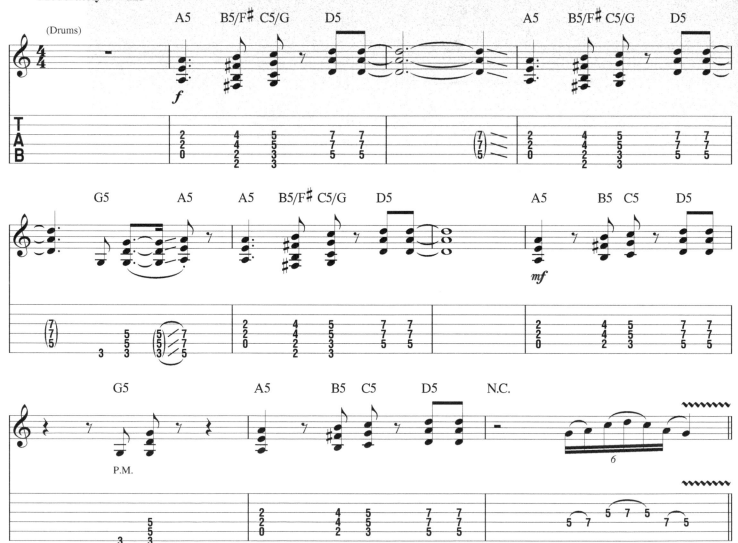

For advanced speed demons only, that quick series of hammer-ons and pull-offs in the last measure is a *sextuplet*—six notes in the space of one beat. Fret each fifth-fret note with your index finger, and each seventh-fret note with your ring finger. Add some fast vibrato on the last note.

Inversions are great thickeners, but they can also be used to "thin out" power chords. Take a three-note G5, for instance:

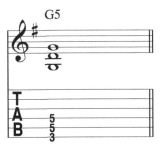

Remove its root, and you're left with a two-note G5/D chord. The 5th, D, is the lowest note; the root, G, is the highest note:

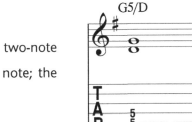

As originally played by Ritchie Blackmore, Deep Purple's "Smoke on the Water" riff features two-note inversions along the fourth and fifth strings. You've probably heard it played—the wrong way—in guitar stores everywhere!

Smoke on the Water

Words and Music by Ritchie Blackmore, Ian Gillan, Roger Glover, Jon Lord and Ian Paice

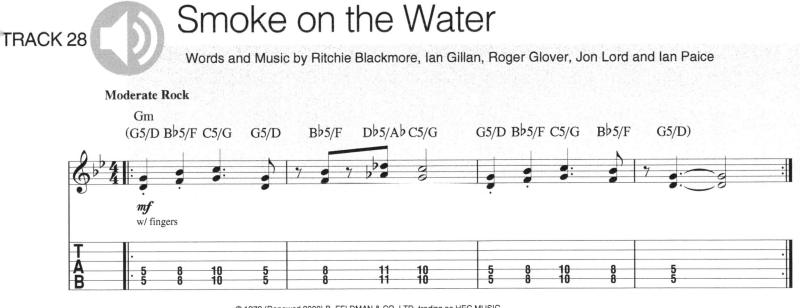

To play this faithfully, pick with your fingers: use your thumb for all fifth-string notes, and your index or middle finger for all fourth-string notes. Use an index-finger barre for the G5/D and B♭5/F chords, and a ring-finger barre for the C5/G and D♭5/A♭ chords.

CHAPTER 5

Power Chords with Surrounding Notes

The Blues

Power chord progressions often incorporate nearby notes from outside the chord. A typical blues shuffle alternates between root-5th and root-6th *dyads* (two-note groupings). Conveniently, the 6th is located two frets above the 5th.

Take a two-note open E5 chord, and without lifting your index finger, fret the fifth string, fourth fret C♯.

E6

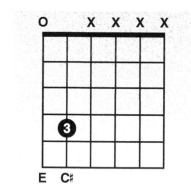

Now try transforming an A5 chord to an A6 chord; just use the same fingering on strings 5–4.

Next, try the same move with a closed-position B5 chord. Keep your index and third fingers down while you fret the fourth string, sixth fret G♯ with your pinky.

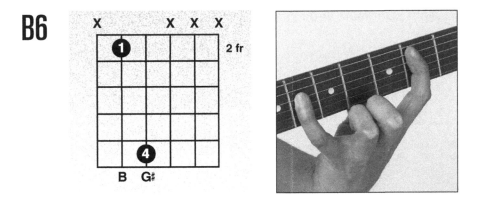

B6

This might feel uncomfortable at first, but keep at it. The fingering is essential for blues and rock riffs. (Some players use the second finger instead of the third, so the pinky stretch is easier.)

Now try an open shuffle pattern. Start by dividing each beat evenly into three parts, counting, "one-uh-*let*, two-uh-*let*, three-uh-*let*, four-uh-*let*," etc. The *swing indicator* (♫ = ♩♪) above the staff means that the pattern's eighth notes are not played evenly; each note falls either on a beat or a "let" (this is also known as *triplet feel*). If this is confusing, just play along with the track; you'll feel the difference between this and a "straight" pattern.

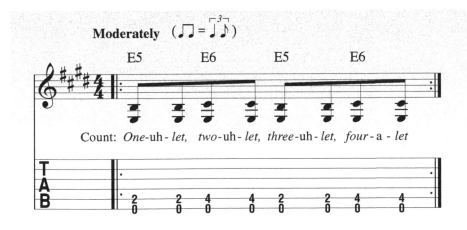

Moderately (♫ = ♩♪)

Once you have the shuffle down, try a complete 12-bar blues form, counting as you did on the previous example. Note that the "and" (in this case, "let") of each beat can be played as a power chord instead of a 6th dyad. Try this with and without a slight palm mute throughout.

TRACK 29

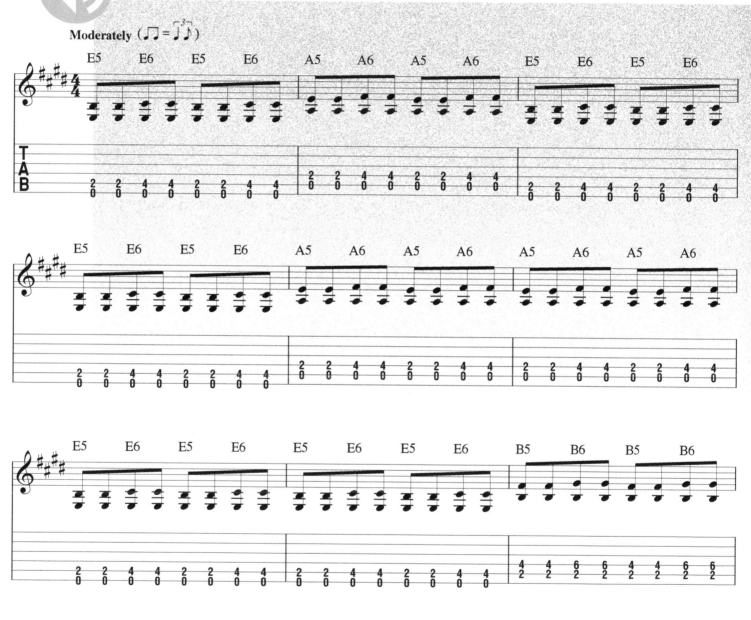

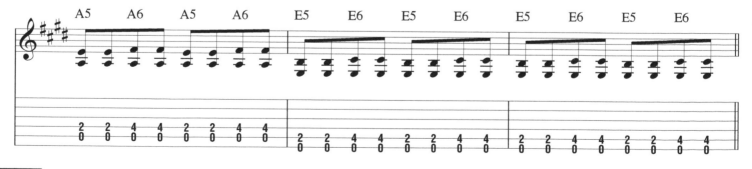

A variation on the basic shuffle pattern pairs the root with the sixth and the *flatted 7th*. The ♭7 is located one fret above the 6th.

With both your index and ring fingers depressed on an E6 dyad, finger fret 5 on the fifth string (D) with your pinky. Now you're implying an E7 chord (E–G♯–B–D).

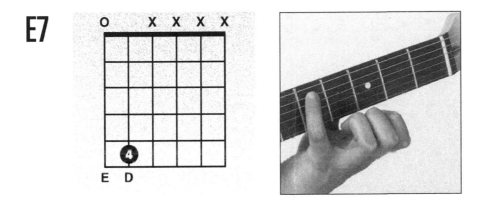

Do the same thing on strings 5–4, forming an A6 leading to an A7 dyad.

The B7 dyad calls for a trickier stretch: First, try fretting the 5th (fourth string, fourth fret F♯) with your middle finger (instead of your ring finger), then planting your pinky finger at the seventh fret:

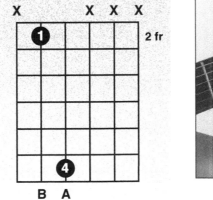

Now we're ready to use the ♭7 in a full 12-bar blues form. Take it slowly at first. Experiment with your fingering, so that you can hit the 6 and ♭7 cleanly without putting too much strain on your hands. Again, try this with slight palm muting throughout.

TRACK 30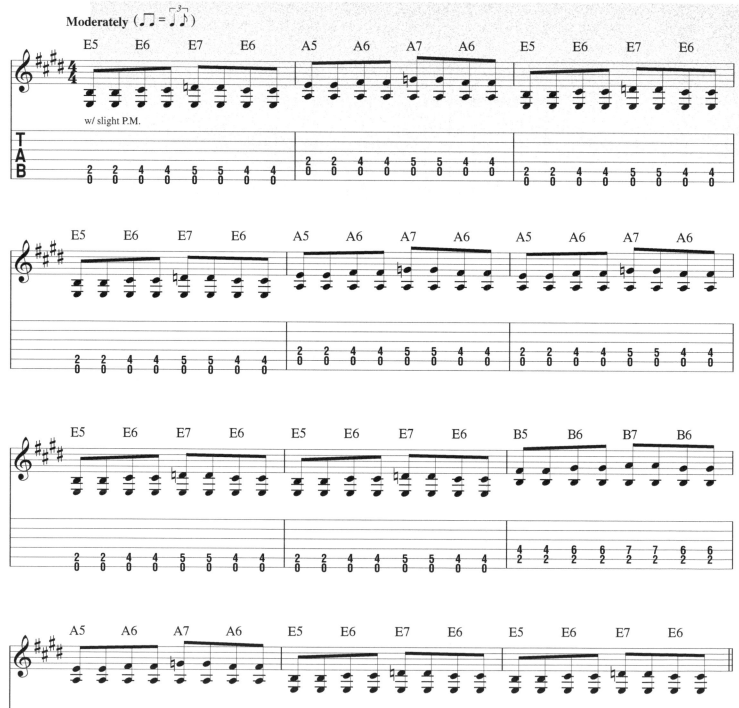

The blues form can be played entirely in closed chord positions, so you easily can move it to any key.

Here are the three patterns for a blues in the key of B♭ major. For each dyad, use the same fingering as you used on the B5–B6–B7 pattern; just move it to the appropriate string and fret.

The Roman numerals above the staff indicate that B♭ is the I chord, E♭ is the IV chord, and F is the V chord. (You'll be using these in the next exercise.)

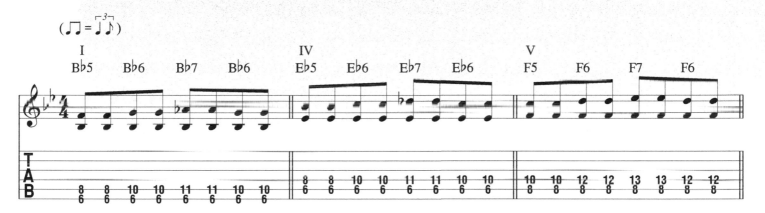

Here is a simple "roadmap" chart of the 12-bar blues, into which you can plug the appropriate patterns in any key. Play the I, IV, and V chord patterns where shown. (The IV chord is optional in measure 2.)

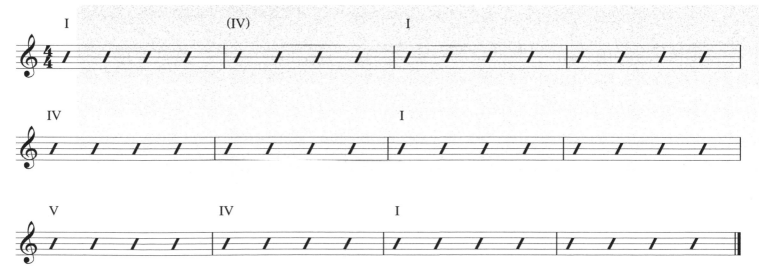

Now try playing these shuffle moves in several other keys. In no time, you'll be able to jam along to hundreds of blues tunes.

The Tritone

Lowering the 5th of any power chord by a half step (one fret) creates a harsh sound—a chordal tritone. Let's try this with a two-note G5 chord. Start with a regular, two-note fingering on the third fret:

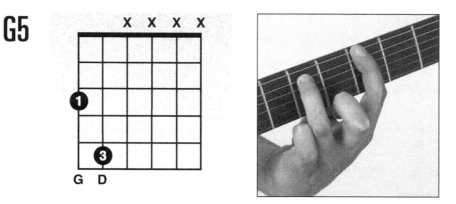

Place your middle finger on the fifth string, fourth fret D♭, and release your ring finger. You now have a dark, dissonant G(♭5) chord.

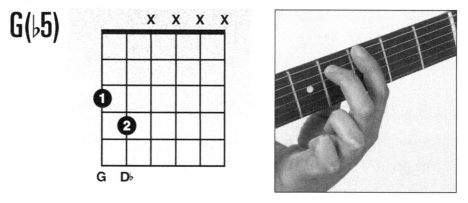

On the staff below, closed power chords rooted on the fifth–second strings are converted to these *flatted 5th* chords. All use the same fingering except for the B♭(♭5), which is best played with your pinky finger on the 5th, and your ring finger on the flatted 5th.

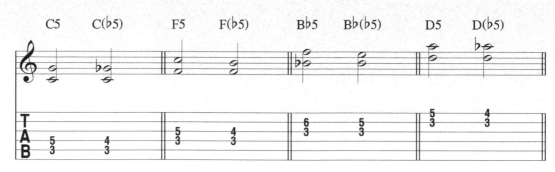

Play these pairs at various other locations along the guitar neck.

This figure, inspired by Joe Satriani, features D(♭5) chords and C(♭5) chords. Listen to how each dissonant ♭5 calls for resolution to the consonant (restful sounding) ♮5.

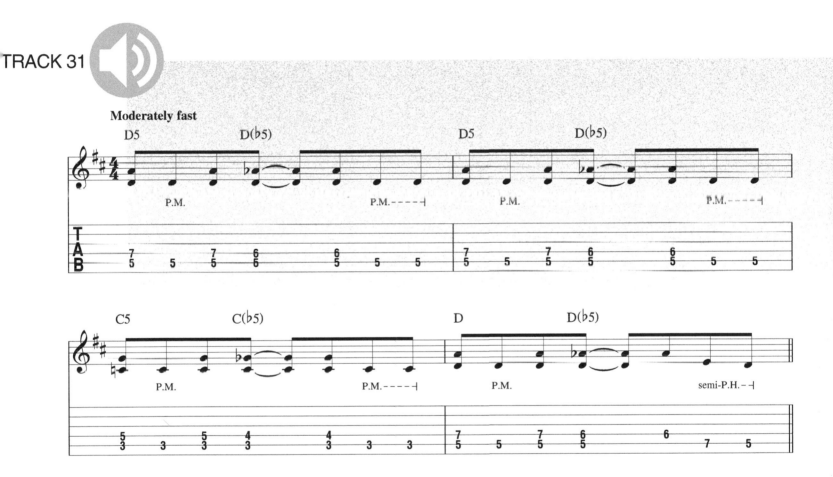

For the "semi-P.H." notes, add a bit of your thumb or index finger to the pick attack to create higher, squealing tones (*pinch harmonics*) along with the fretted pitches. This technique takes some time to develop; experiment until you get the right sound.

Lowering the Root

You can also create new sounds by lowering a power chord's root by a half step. You'll hear this most often on fifth-string rooted chords. Start with a two-note E5 chord, but use your pinky finger to fret the 5th.

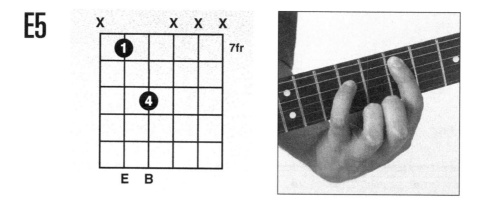

E5

Now you can easily move your index finger to the fifth string, sixth fret D♯, forming a B/D♯ chord. (The root of the B triad is the higher note; the 5th, F♯, is implied.)

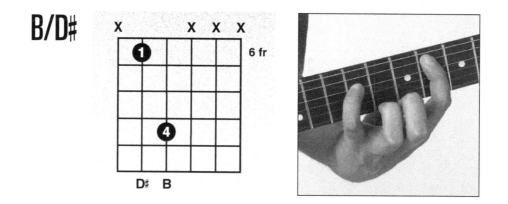

B/D♯

You can also lower the root of a D5 by a half step to form an A/C♯ chord.

This figure features these power chord/inverted triad pairs above an E pedal tone (a constant, unchanging bass note), resolving on an open E5 chord.

TRACK 32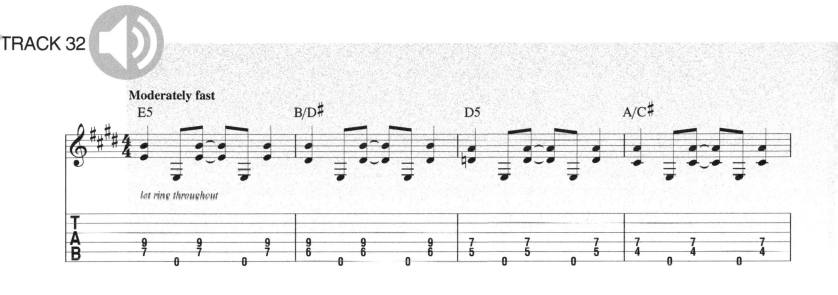

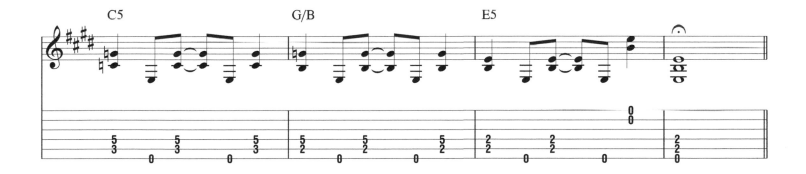

Adding the 3rd

Major- and minor-3rd dyads can also be incorporated in power chord progressions. Here is a diatonic example in the key of E major, made up of of E5, F#5, and A5 chords connected by assorted 3rds, which are named between the staves.

For each minor 3rd (m3), fret the lower note with your ring finger and the higher note with your index finger; for each major 3rd (M3), fret the lower note with your middle finger and the higher note with your index finger.

TRACK 33

Here is the same progression adjusted to E minor. Notice the resulting *inverse* relationship—the previous figure's major 3rds have become minor, and the minor 3rds have become major.

TRACK 34

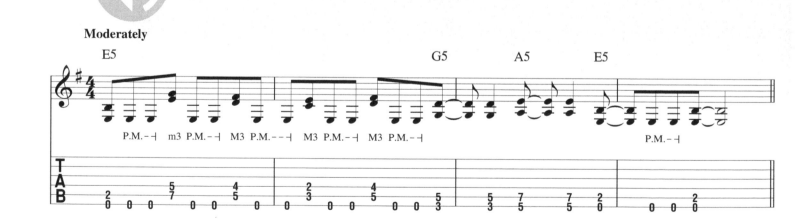

Using non-diatonic 3rds in power chord progressions can create striking effects. In this figure, inspired by Metallica, the D#/F# and C/E♭ dyads contain pitches outside of the E minor key signature. This dissonance, and the tritone progressions of B♭5–E5 and F5–B5, give the pattern a menacing feel. Pick each chord stab with a downstroke; use alternate picking on the palm-muted sixth-string fills.

TRACK 35

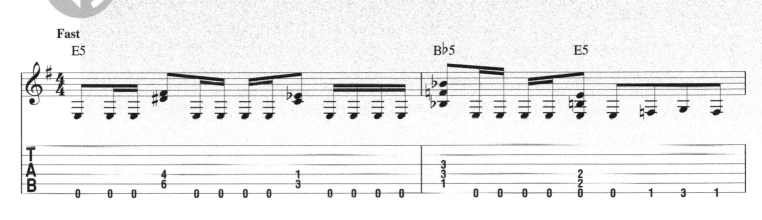

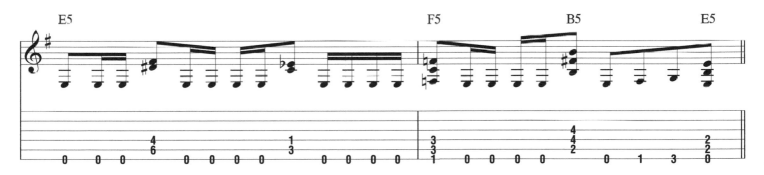

Now try inventing some of your own power chord riffs, incorporating the dyads we used in this chapter. Use both diatonic and chromatic materials, and strive for creativity.

CHAPTER 6

Drop D Power Chords

Some of the most powerful guitar riffs in history are played in *drop D tuning*, which makes it easy to access sixth-string rooted power chords. The sixth string is tuned down a whole step from E to D, so that the sixth, fifth, and fourth strings have a root–5th–octave (D–A–D) relationship. This means that you can play closed-position power chords with one fret-hand finger.

Tune your sixth string down to D. You can do this manually by playing a note (or a harmonic, if you're good with them) on fret 12 of the sixth string, and matching that with the open fourth string. You can also use an electronic tuner or the tuning track:

 **TRACK 36**

TUNING NOTES: D–A–D–G–B–E

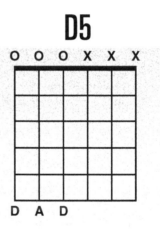

Then, to feel the power of drop D tuning, play an open D5 chord. No fingering is necessary; just play the open sixth, fifth, and fourth strings.

Now try playing drop D power chords from open position up to the twelfth fret. Name the chords as you play them, but note that each sixth-string root is one step (one letter) lower than in standard tuning.

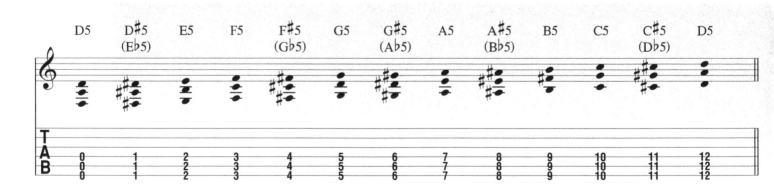

Try barring these chords with all four of your fret-hand fingers—you'll see that the finger used to fret a chord varies according to the situation. You can also play the chords as two-note voicings; just omit the fourth string.

This riff shows some of the articulation techniques that drop D tuning makes possible—entire power chords can be hammered on and pulled off.

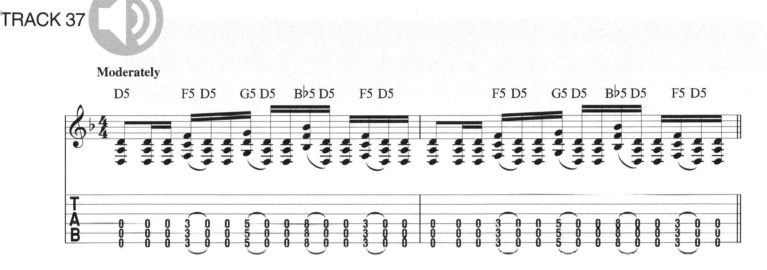

Use your index finger to barre the third-fret F5 chord, and your ring finger to barre the G5 and B♭5 chords. When pulling off, don't use too much force; that can cause the strings to sound sharp.

Soundgarden's "Outshined" riff is in the odd time signature of 7/4, but the feel is straight-ahead rock. Palm mute the first two open D5 chords, then use your index, middle, and pinky fingers for the F5, G5, and A♭5 chords, respectively. The C note on beat 5 gets a dose of vibrato from the index finger (shift from a barre to a single fretted note).

Outshined

Words and Music by Chris Cornell

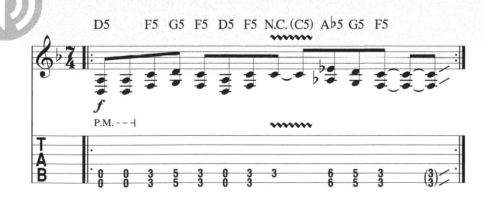

Now that you're counting to seven in grunge mode, try the even odder time signature of 7/8: Alice in Chains' "Them Bones" takes full advantage of drop D power chords. (The original was played in drop D tuning, down one half step; we've adjusted it here to match your tuning.)

TRACK 39

Them Bones

Written by Jerry Cantrell

The first pattern goes up chromatically from an open D5 chord to a third-fret F5 chord. For the D♯5, E5, and F5 chords, experiment to find which fret-hand fingering works best for you. You could play all with an index finger barre, or bar the D♯5, E5, and F5 chords with your index, middle, and ring fingers respectively.

The second pattern features four-note drop D chords. Closed position ones are best played with an index-finger barre on the bottom three notes, and the ring finger fretting the highest note. Try this fingering up and down the guitar neck.

Drop D tuning is not just for rock—in fact, it was first a traditional blues tuning. If you have trouble stretching your fingers to reach the 6th and ♭7 in a blues shuffle, drop D is for you. This riff is a variation on the standard blues lick made famous by Elmore James, juxtaposed with an A5 shuffle pattern.

TRACK 40

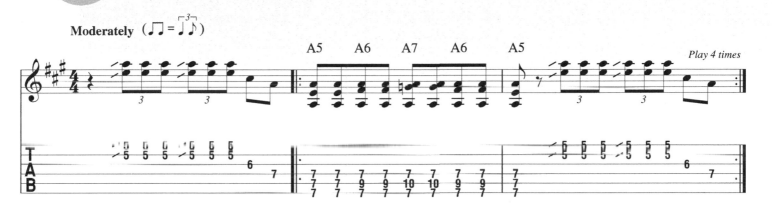

Slide up to the dyad on the high E and B strings with an index-finger barre. After playing the lick, shift your hand so that your index finger is barring the A5 and you can use your ring and pinky fingers for the 6th and ♭7, respectively. Notice the added bluesy dissonance created when you keep the A octave barred over the shuffle pattern.

In drop D tuning, sus2 (*suspended*) chords are sometimes used to add color. What's a sus2 chord? Let's take a C major chord [C–E–G], replace the 3rd (E) with a 2nd (D), and you get a Csus2 chord [C–D–G]. The 2nd is called a *suspension*, because that note tends to resolve to the major 3rd in classical music; hanging on the 2nd keeps us "in suspense" waiting for that to happen.

Here's a three-note sus2 fingering in drop D tuning. The 2nd is fretted with the ring finger:

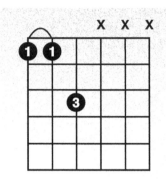

And here's a four-note version, which reinforces the 5th with an octave:

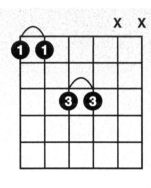

Once you're comfortable with these new fingerings, try them in context:

TRACK 41

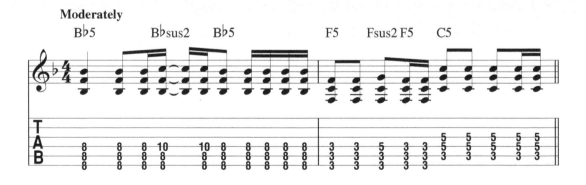

Use an index-finger barre for the B♭5 and F5 chords. To create each sus2 chord, just add your ring finger on the highest note. And as the C5 chord shows, fifth-string rooted power chords are fingered the same in drop D as in standard tuning.

You can also play this example with four-note voicings in this alternative fingering. Use your pinky finger on the highest note as shown. That leaves your ring finger free to fret each suspended 2nd when the time comes.

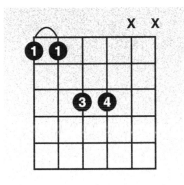

Now try the same progression with four-note chords—notice the new position for the C5.

TRACK 42

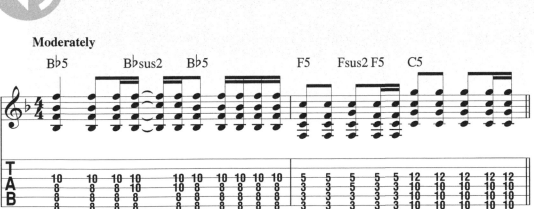

In drop-D power chord progressions, octaves are often inserted for textural variety. As we said earlier, an octave incorporates two of the same notes, twelve half steps apart. Here are some "pure" octave shapes rooted on the 5th, 4th, and 3rd strings, respectively. You can think of these octaves as three-note power chords, without the 5ths. In each, the backside of your index finger mutes the middle string, marked in frames and tablature with an "X."

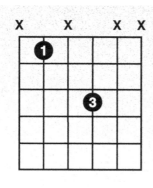

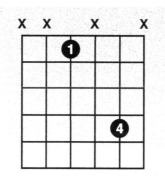

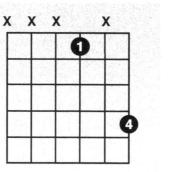

This figure features a typical pattern of octaves alternated with three-note, open D5 chords. Pick your left hand off the neck for the muted open chords, and make sure the middle string between your octaves is completely muted. Listen for the differences between the octaves and power chords—the octaves stand out, creating a melodic line.

TRACK 43

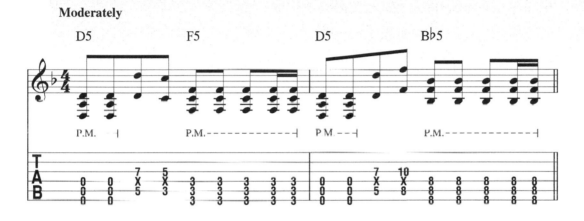

Modern rock bands often use ultra-low variations of drop D tuning. Combined with heavy overdrive, this gives you serious crunch and earth-shaking low end. If you want to do this often, use heavier strings to keep your intonation steady; in these lower tunings, standard- or light-guage strings will flop around and sound sharp, ring against the frets, and go out of tune. For now, try bringing your drop D tuning down one step for the next example.

TRACK 44

DROP D TUNING, DOWN 1 STEP: (LOW TO HIGH) C–G–C–F–A–D

In lowered tunings like this, songs are usually transcribed as if they're in regular drop D tuning; in other words, your open D5 power chord is still written as a D5, even though it's really a C5.

System of a Down's "Aerials" features both sus2 chords and octaves. The B♭sus2 chords on beat 4 of measures 1 and 2 are ornamental. In the third and fourth measures, palm-muted, open D5 chords are alternated with octaves along the 5th string for a dramatic, descending line.

TRACK 45

Aerials

Words and Music by Daron Malakian and Serj Tankian

Drop D tuning, down 1 step:
(low to high) C-G-C-F-A-D

Moderately slow Rock ♩ = 80

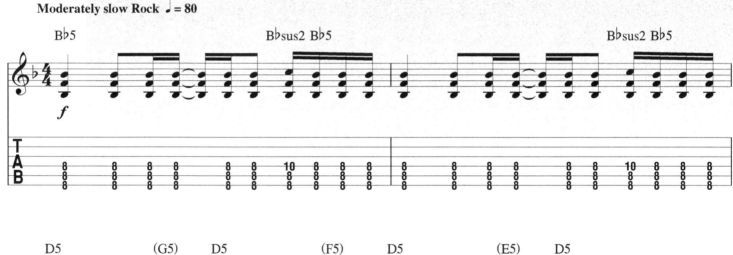

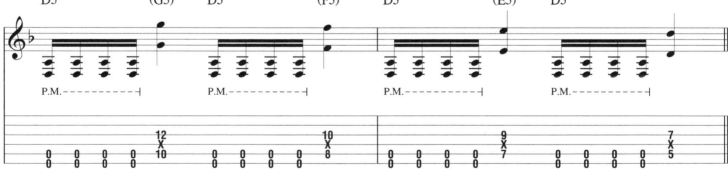

APPENDIX
Fretboard Chart

This chart displays all of the available pitches on the fretboard. Two pitches shown together are called *enharmonic,* meaning they are two different note names for the same pitch.

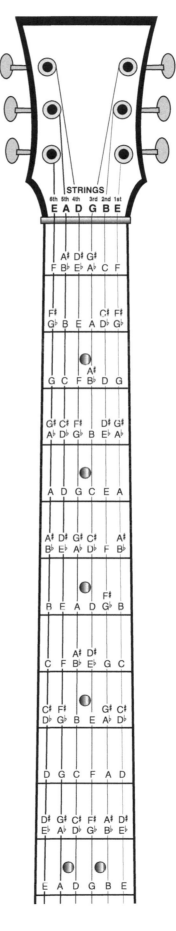

Reading Chord Diagrams

A chord diagram represents a chunk of the guitar's neck, and indicates the notes and fingerings of a particular chord, which is named on top. The horizontal lines are frets and the vertical lines symbolize strings (as if the guitar neck is pointing up). A number to the right of a frame shows the fret position; "10 fr" means the diagram starts at fret 10. In open position, you'll see a thick horizontal line on top that represents the guitar nut (where the neck meets the headstock). An "O" above a frame indicates an open string, and an "X" calls for a string to be muted or left unplayed. Dots on the diagram are fingerings, and a *barre*, the curvy line above fingerings, indicates that the given strings are to be held down with the same finger. Inside the dots are numbers that explain which fret-hand fingers to use: 1=index, 2=middle, 3=ring, and 4=pinky.

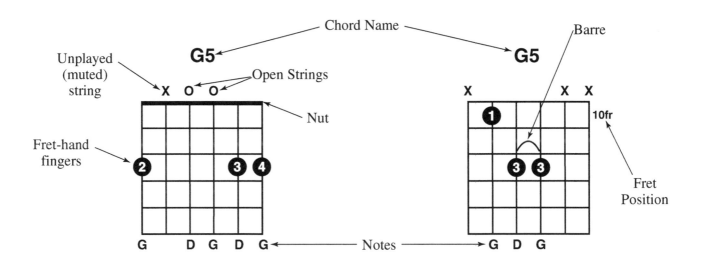

Reading Tablature

Tablature (or *tab*) is another representation of the guitar's fretboard, showing the string and fret coordinates of any note. The six horizontal lines represent strings: the bottom line is the low E string, and the highest is the high E string. While tablature is extremely helpful in terms of positioning, it is not meant to replace standard notation.

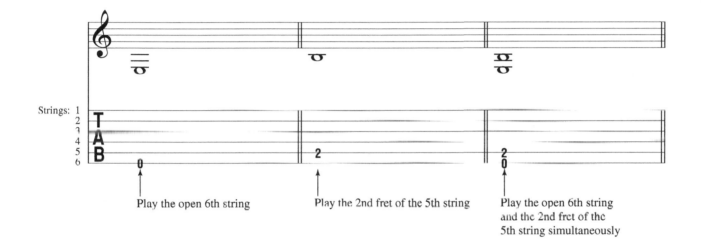

Play the open 6th string   Play the 2nd fret of the 5th string   Play the open 6th string and the 2nd fret of the 5th string simultaneously

GUITAR NOTATION LEGEND

Guitar music can be notated three different ways: on a *musical staff*, in *tablature*, and in *rhythm slashes*.

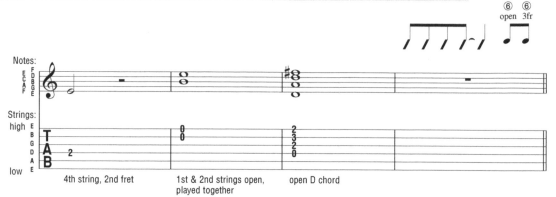

RHYTHM SLASHES are written above the staff. Strum chords in the rhythm indicated. Use the chord diagrams found at the top of the first page of the transcription for the appropriate chord voicings. Round noteheads indicate single notes.

THE MUSICAL STAFF shows pitches and rhythms and is divided by bar lines into measures. Pitches are named after the first seven letters of the alphabet.

TABLATURE graphically represents the guitar fingerboard. Each horizontal line represents a string, and each number represents a fret.

4th string, 2nd fret   1st & 2nd strings open, played together   open D chord

---

HALF-STEP BEND: Strike the note and bend up 1/2 step.

WHOLE-STEP BEND: Strike the note and bend up one step.

GRACE NOTE BEND: Strike the note and immediately bend up as indicated.

SLIGHT (MICROTONE) BEND: Strike the note and bend up 1/4 step.

BEND AND RELEASE: Strike the note and bend up as indicated, then release back to the original note. Only the first note is struck.

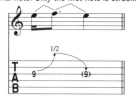

PRE-BEND: Bend the note as indicated, then strike it.

VIBRATO: The string is vibrated by rapidly bending and releasing the note with the fretting hand.

WIDE VIBRATO: The pitch is varied to a greater degree by vibrating with the fretting hand.

HAMMER-ON: Strike the first (lower) note with one finger, then sound the higher note (on the same string) with another finger by fretting it without picking.

PULL-OFF: Place both fingers on the notes to be sounded. Strike the first note and without picking, pull the finger off to sound the second (lower) note.

LEGATO SLIDE: Strike the first note and then slide the same fret-hand finger up or down to the second note. The second note is not struck.

SHIFT SLIDE: Same as legato slide, except the second note is struck.

TRILL: Very rapidly alternate between the notes indicated by continuously hammering on and pulling off.

TAPPING: Hammer ("tap") the fret indicated with the pick-hand index or middle finger and pull off to the note fretted by the fret hand.

NATURAL HARMONIC: Strike the note while the fret-hand lightly touches the string directly over the fret indicated.

PINCH HARMONIC: The note is fretted normally and a harmonic is produced by adding the edge of the thumb or the tip of the index finger of the pick hand to the normal pick attack.

PICK SCRAPE: The edge of the pick is rubbed down (or up) the string, producing a scratchy sound.

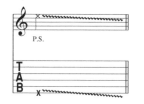

MUFFLED STRINGS: A percussive sound is produced by laying the fret hand across the string(s) without depressing, and striking them with the pick hand.

PALM MUTING: The note is partially muted by the pick hand lightly touching the string(s) just before the bridge.

RAKE: Drag the pick across the strings indicated with a single motion.

TREMOLO PICKING: The note is picked as rapidly and continuously as possible.

VIBRATO BAR DIVE AND RETURN: The pitch of the note or chord is dropped a specified number of steps (in rhythm), then returned to the original pitch.

VIBRATO BAR SCOOP: Depress the bar just before striking the note, then quickly release the bar.

VIBRATO BAR DIP: Strike the note and then immediately drop a specified number of steps, then release back to the original pitch.

Get Better at Guitar

...with these Great Guitar Instruction Books from Hal Leonard!

101 GUITAR TIPS
INCLUDES TAB

STUFF ALL THE PROS KNOW AND USE

by Adam St. James

This book contains invaluable guidance on everything from scales and music theory to truss rod adjustments, proper recording studio set-ups, and much more. The book also features snippets of advice from some of the most celebrated guitarists and producers in the music business, including B.B. King, Steve Vai, Joe Satriani, Warren Haynes, Laurence Juber, Pete Anderson, Tom Dowd and others, culled from the author's hundreds of interviews.

00695737 Book/Online Audio $16.99

AMAZING PHRASING
INCLUDES TAB

50 WAYS TO IMPROVE YOUR IMPROVISATIONAL SKILLS

by Tom Kolb

This book/audio pack explores all the main components necessary for crafting well-balanced rhythmic and melodic phrases. It also explains how these phrases are put together to form cohesive solos. Many styles are covered – rock, blues, jazz, fusion, country, Latin, funk and more – and all of the concepts are backed up with musical examples. The companion audio contains 89 demos for listening, and most tracks feature full-band backing.

00695583 Book/Online Audio $19.99

BLUES YOU CAN USE – 2ND EDITION

by John Ganapes

This comprehensive source for learning blues guitar is designed to develop both your lead and rhythm playing. Includes: 21 complete solos • blues chords, progressions and riffs • turnarounds • movable scales and soloing techniques • string bending • utilizing the entire fingerboard • and more. This second edition now includes audio and video access online!

00142420 Book/Online Media...................................$19.99

FRETBOARD MASTERY
INCLUDES TAB

by Troy Stetina

Untangle the mysterious regions of the guitar fretboard and unlock your potential. *Fretboard Mastery* familiarizes you with all the shapes you need to know by applying them in real musical examples, thereby reinforcing and reaffirming your newfound knowledge. The result is a much higher level of comprehension and retention.

00695331 Book/Online Audio $19.99

FRETBOARD ROADMAPS – 2ND EDITION

ESSENTIAL GUITAR PATTERNS THAT ALL THE PROS KNOW AND USE

by Fred Sokolow

The updated edition of this bestseller features more songs, updated lessons, audio tracks! Learn to play lead and rhythm anywhere on the fretboard, in any key; play a variety of lead guitar styles; play chords and progressions anywhere on the fretboard; expand your chord vocabulary; and learn to think musically – the way the pros do.

00695941 Book/Online Audio $15.99

GUITAR AEROBICS
INCLUDES TAB

A 52-WEEK, ONE-LICK-PER-DAY WORKOUT PROGRAM FOR DEVELOPING, IMPROVING & MAINTAINING GUITAR TECHNIQUE

by Troy Nelson

From the former editor of *Guitar One* magazine, here is a daily dose of vitamins to keep your chops fine tuned! Musical styles include rock, blues, jazz, metal, country, and funk. Techniques taught include alternate picking, arpeggios, sweep picking, string skipping, legato, string bending, and rhythm guitar. These exercises will increase speed, and improve dexterity and pick- and fret-hand accuracy. The accompanying audio includes all 365 workout licks plus play-along grooves in every style at eight different metronome settings.

00695946 Book/Online Audio $19.99

GUITAR CLUES
INCLUDES TAB

OPERATION PENTATONIC

by Greg Koch

Join renowned guitar master Greg Koch as he clues you in to a wide variety of fun and valuable pentatonic scale applications. Whether you're new to improvising or have been doing it for a while, this book/audio pack will provide loads of delicious licks and tricks that you can use right away, from volume swells and chicken pickin' to intervallic and chordal ideas. The online audio includes 65 demo and play-along tracks.

00695827 Book/Online Audio $19.99

INTRODUCTION TO GUITAR TONE & EFFECTS

by David M. Brewster

This book/audio pack teaches the basics of guitar tones and effects, with online audio examples. Readers will learn about: overdrive, distortion and fuzz • using equalizers • modulation effects • reverb and delay • multi-effect processors • and more.

00695766 Book/Online Audio $16.99

PICTURE CHORD ENCYCLOPEDIA

This comprehensive guitar chord resource for all playing styles and levels features five voicings of 44 chord qualities for all twelve keys – 2,640 chords in all! For each, there is a clearly illustrated chord frame, as well as *an actual photo* of the chord being played! Includes info on basic fingering principles, open chords and barre chords, partial chords and broken-set forms, and more.

00695224...$19.95

SCALE CHORD RELATIONSHIPS
INCLUDES TAB

by Michael Mueller & Jeff Schroedl

This book teaches players how to determine which scales to play with which chords, so guitarists will never have to fear chord changes again! This book/audio pack explains how to: recognize keys • analyze chord progressions • use the modes • play over nondiatonic harmony • use harmonic and melodic minor scales • use symmetrical scales such as chromatic, whole-tone and diminished scales • incorporate exotic scales such as Hungarian major and Gypsy minor • and much more!

00695563 Book/Online Audio $14.99

SPEED MECHANICS FOR LEAD GUITAR
INCLUDES TAB

Take your playing to the stratosphere with the most advanced lead book by this proven heavy metal author. *Speed Mechanics* is the ultimate technique book for developing the kind of speed and precision in today's explosive playing styles. Learn the fastest ways to achieve speed and control, secrets to make your practice time really count, and how to open your ears and make your musical ideas more solid and tangible. Packed with over 200 vicious exercises including Troy's scorching version of "Flight of the Bumblebee." Music and examples demonstrated on the accompanying online audio.

00699323 Book/Online Audio $19.99

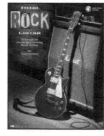

TOTAL ROCK GUITAR
INCLUDES TAB

A COMPLETE GUIDE TO LEARNING ROCK GUITAR

by Troy Stetina

This unique and comprehensive source for learning rock guitar is designed to develop both lead and rhythm playing. It covers: getting a tone that rocks • open chords, power chords and barre chords • riffs, scales and licks • string bending, strumming, palm muting, harmonics and alternate picking • all rock styles • and much more. The examples are in standard notation with chord grids and tab, and the audio includes full-band backing for all 22 songs.

00695246 Book/Online Audio $19.99

Visit Hal Leonard Online at
www.halleonard.com

Prices, contents, and availability subject to change without notice.

0319
032

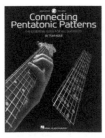

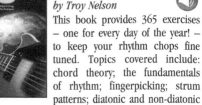

GUITAR *signature licks*

AC/DC
14041352.....................$22.99

AEROSMITH 1973-1979
00695106.....................$22.95

AEROSMITH 1979-1998
00695219.....................$22.95

DUANE ALLMAN
00696042.....................$22.99

BEST OF CHET ATKINS
00695752.....................$24.99

AVENGED SEVENFOLD
00696473.....................$22.99

THE BEATLES
00298845.....................$24.99

BEST OF THE BEATLES FOR ACOUSTIC GUITAR
00695453.....................$22.99

THE BEATLES HITS
00695049.....................$24.95

JEFF BECK
00696427.....................$22.99

BEST OF GEORGE BENSON
00695418.....................$22.99

BEST OF BLACK SABBATH
00695249.....................$22.95

BLUES BREAKERS WITH JOHN MAYALL & ERIC CLAPTON
00696374.....................$24.99

BON JOVI
00696380.....................$22.99

ROY BUCHANAN
00696654.....................$22.99

KENNY BURRELL
00695830.....................$24.99

BEST OF CHARLIE CHRISTIAN
00695584.....................$24.99

BEST OF ERIC CLAPTON
00695038.....................$24.99

ERIC CLAPTON – FROM THE ALBUM UNPLUGGED
00695250.....................$24.99

BEST OF CREAM
00695251.....................$22.95

CREEDANCE CLEARWATER REVIVAL
00695924.....................$24.99

THE DOORS
00695373.....................$22.95

DEEP PURPLE – GREATEST HITS
00695625.....................$22.99

DREAM THEATER
00111943.....................$24.99

TOMMY EMMANUEL
00696409.....................$22.99

ESSENTIAL JAZZ GUITAR
00695875.....................$19.99

FAMOUS ROCK GUITAR SOLOS
00695590.....................$19.95

FLEETWOOD MAC
00696416.....................$22.99

BEST OF FOO FIGHTERS
00695481.....................$24.95

ROBBEN FORD
00695903.....................$22.95

BEST OF GRANT GREEN
00695747.....................$22.99

PETER GREEN
00145386.....................$22.99

BEST OF GUNS N' ROSES
00695183.....................$24.99

THE BEST OF BUDDY GUY
00695186.....................$22.99

JIM HALL
00695848.....................$29.99

JIMI HENDRIX
00696560.....................$24.99

JIMI HENDRIX – VOLUME 2
00695835.....................$24.99

JOHN LEE HOOKER
00695894.....................$22.99

BEST OF JAZZ GUITAR
00695586.....................$29.99

ERIC JOHNSON
00699317.....................$24.99

ROBERT JOHNSON
00695264.....................$24.99

BARNEY KESSEL
00696009.....................$24.99

THE ESSENTIAL ALBERT KING
00695713.....................$24.99

B.B. KING – BLUES LEGEND
00696039.....................$22.99

B.B. KING – THE DEFINITIVE COLLECTION
00695635.....................$22.99

MARK KNOPFLER
00695178.....................$24.99

LYNYRD SKYNYRD
00695872.....................$24.99

THE BEST OF YNGWIE MALMSTEEN
00695669.....................$24.99

BEST OF PAT MARTINO
00695632.....................$24.99

MEGADETH
00696421.....................$22.99

WES MONTGOMERY
00695387.....................$24.99

BEST OF NIRVANA
00695483.....................$24.95

VERY BEST OF OZZY OSBOURNE
00695431.....................$22.99

BRAD PAISLEY
00696379.....................$22.99

BEST OF JOE PASS
00695730.....................$22.99

TOM PETTY
00696021.....................$22.99

PINK FLOYD
00103659.....................$24.99

THE GUITAR OF ELVIS
00174800.....................$22.99

BEST OF QUEEN
00695097.....................$24.99

RADIOHEAD
00109304.....................$24.99

BEST OF RAGE AGAINST THE MACHINE
00695480.....................$24.95

RED HOT CHILI PEPPERS
00695173.....................$22.95

RED HOT CHILI PEPPERS – GREATEST HITS
00695828.....................$24.99

JERRY REED
00118236.....................$22.99

BEST OF DJANGO REINHARDT
00695660.....................$24.99

BEST OF ROCK 'N' ROLL GUITAR
00695559.....................$22.99

BEST OF ROCKABILLY GUITAR
00695785.....................$19.99

BEST OF CARLOS SANTANA
00174664.....................$22.99

BEST OF JOE SATRIANI
00695216.....................$22.95

SLASH
00696576.....................$22.99

SLAYER
00121281.....................$22.99

THE BEST OF SOUL GUITAR
00695703.....................$19.95

BEST OF SOUTHERN ROCK
00695560.....................$19.95

STEELY DAN
00696015.....................$22.99

MIKE STERN
00695800.....................$24.99

BEST OF SURF GUITAR
00695822.....................$19.99

STEVE VAI
00673247.....................$24.99

STEVE VAI – ALIEN LOVE SECRETS: THE NAKED VAMPS
00695223.....................$22.95

STEVE VAI – FIRE GARDEN: THE NAKED VAMPS
00695166.....................$22.95

STEVE VAI – THE ULTRA ZONE: NAKED VAMPS
00695684.....................$22.95

VAN HALEN
00110227.....................$24.99

STEVIE RAY VAUGHAN – 2ND ED.
00699316.....................$24.95

THE GUITAR STYLE OF STEVIE RAY VAUGHAN
00695155.....................$24.95

BEST OF THE VENTURES
00695772.....................$19.95

THE WHO – 2ND ED.
00695561.....................$22.95

JOHNNY WINTER
00695951.....................$24.99

YES
00113120.....................$22.99

NEIL YOUNG – GREATEST HITS
00695988.....................$22.99

BEST OF ZZ TOP
00695738.....................$24.99

HAL•LEONARD®

www.halleonard.com

COMPLETE DESCRIPTIONS AND SONGLISTS ONLINE!
Prices, contents and availability subject to change without notice.